Stay Safe!

On the road

Lisa Bruce

Heinemann
LIBRARY

Little Nippers

www.heinemann.co.uk/library
Visit our website to find out more information about **Heinemann Library** books.

To order:
☎ Phone 44 (0) 1865 888066
🖹 Send a fax to 44 (0) 1865 314091
 Visit the Heinemann Bookshop at www.heinemann.co.uk/library to browse our catalogue and order online.

First published in Great Britain by Heinemann Library, Halley Court, Jordan Hill, Oxford OX2 8EJ, part of Harcourt Education.
Heinemann is a registered trademark of Harcourt Education Ltd.

Editorial: Jilly Attwood and Claire Throp
Design: Jo Hinton-Malivoire and bigtop, Bicester, UK
Models made by: Jo Brooker
Picture Research: Rosie Garai
Production: Séverine Ribierre

Originated by Dot Gradations
Printed and bound in China by South China Printing Company

ISBN 0 431 17271 4 (hardback)
07 06 05 04 03
10 9 8 7 6 5 4 3 2 1

ISBN 0 431 17276 5 (paperback)
07 06 05 04 03
10 9 8 7 6 5 4 3 2 1

British Library Cataloguing in Publication Data
Bruce, Lisa
Stay safe on the road – (Little Nippers)
363.1'257
A full catalogue record for this book is available from the British Library.

Acknowledgements
The publishers would like to thank the following for permission to reproduce photographs:
Collections pp. **12**, **17** (Paul Bryans), **13** (Gordon Hill), 21 (Nigel French); Gareth Boden pp. **4–5**, **6**, **7**, **8**, **10–11**, **22–23**; Image State p. **19** (David Lissy); Tudor Photography pp. **13** bottom, **14–15**.

Cover photograph reproduced with permission of Angela Hampton.

The publishers would like to thank Annie Davy for her assistance in the preparation of this book.

Every effort has been made to contact copyright holders of any material reproduced in this book. Any omissions will be rectified in subsequent printings if notice is given to the publishers.

Contents

Safety on the road

Do you like going out for a walk?

To stay safe there are a few things you need to watch out for.

Stay on the pavement

Cars **zoom** along the road very *fast*.

Where should you walk?

On the pavement.

Hold hands

The best way to stay safe is to always hold hands with a grown-up, like your mum and dad or your teacher.

STAY SAFE

Playing near roads

BOing

Darren has dropped his ball.

Should he run after it?

NO!

Cross safely

crossing patrol
assistant

Look both ways!

Listen for traffic!

subway

Walk, don't run!

pelican crossing

13

Say NO to strangers

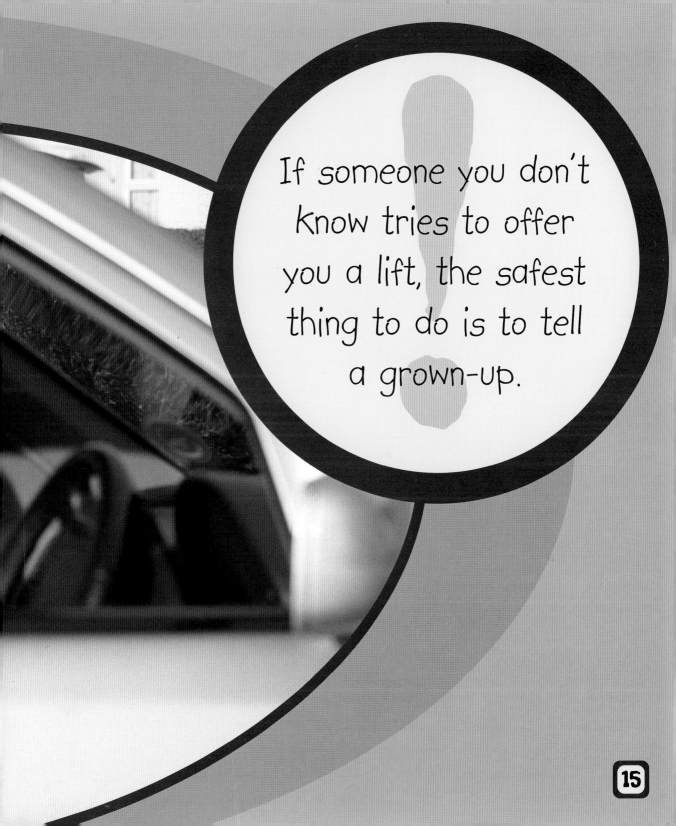

If someone you don't know tries to offer you a lift, the safest thing to do is to tell a grown-up.

Wear reflective clothing

Cars can see light colours best in the **dark**.

Protect yourself

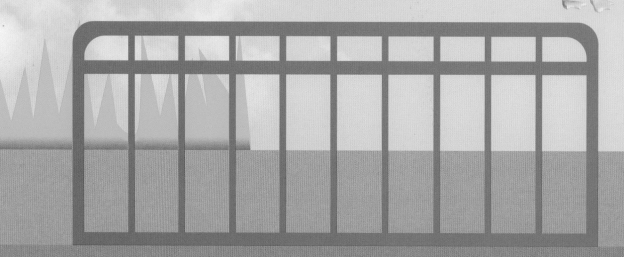

Matthew is wearing a helmet to keep him safe on his bike.

19

The police

Who is around to make sure that you stay safe?

The police

Follow the rules

Follow these rules
Make a start
You'll stay safe
And you'll be smart!

Index

The end

Notes for adults

Stay Safe! supports young children's knowledge and understanding of the world around them. The four books will help children to connect safely with the ever-expanding world in which they find themselves. The following Early Learning Goals are relevant to this series:
• move with confidence, imagination and in safety
• move with control and co-ordination
• show awareness of space, of themselves and of others
• use a range of small and large equipment
• handle tools, objects, construction and malleable materials safely and with increasing control
• understand what is right, what is wrong, and why
• dress and undress independently and manage their own personal hygiene.

The *Stay Safe!* series will help children to think more about the potential dangers they will face as they grow up. Discussion can be focused on what makes an activity safe or unsafe allowing the children to learn how to protect themselves from harm. The books can be used to help children understand how their own behaviour can make a difference to their safety.

On the road will help children extend their vocabulary, as they will hear new words such as *pavement*, *subway*, *pelican crossing*, *assistant*, *strangers*, *reflective*, *protect*, *helmet* and *police*.

Follow-up activities
• Cut strips of material: dark, light and reflective. In a darkened room, shine a light on to the different materials and ask which one shows up more in the light. Discuss how this could be used to help the children stay safe on the road.
• Draw a layout of a road system on a large sheet of paper or card including crossing points and pavements. Ask how to get from one point to another safely.

Lawrence has Nits

A DOCTOR SPOT CASE BOOK

For Sarah

First published in the UK in 2003 by
Red Kite Books, an imprint of Haldane Mason Ltd
PO Box 34196, London NW10 3YB
email: info@haldanemason.com

ISBN 1-902463-90-0

A HALDANE MASON BOOK

Colour reproduction by Smart Solutions Ltd, UK

Printed in the UAE

Please note:
The information presented in this book is intended as a support to
professional advice and care. It is not a substitute for medical diagnosis or
treatment. Always notify and consult your doctor if your child is ill.

"The Patients Association recognize the need for literature on children's
health that is educational and enjoyable for both the child and parent.
We welcome the publication of this Doctor Spot Case Book."

Lawrence has Nits

Jenny Leigh

Illustrated by Woody Fox

ReD KiTE

4

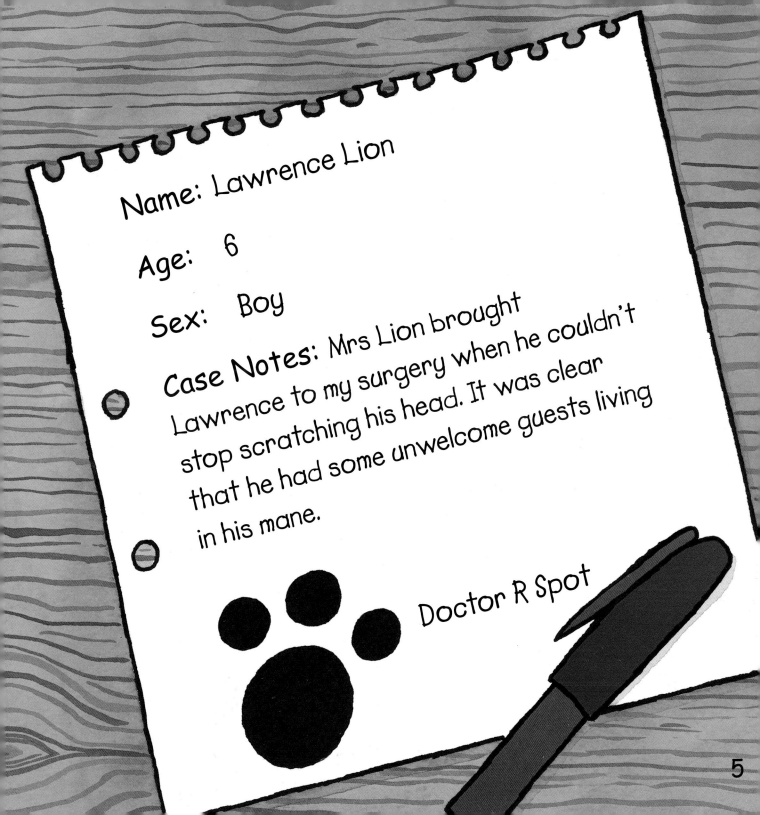

Lawrence was going to the barber to have his mane trimmed. Lawrence wanted his mane to grow long and shaggy like his Dad's, but Mrs Lion liked him to have it trimmed once in a while to take off the split ends and make it easier to comb.

"Hurry up and eat your breakfast," said Mrs Lion. "You don't want to keep Mr Monkey waiting."

Lawrence walked to Mr Monkey's barber shop.

"Hello Lawrence," said Mr Monkey. "Jump up here and let me wash your hair." Lawrence hung his head over the basin and Mr Monkey washed his hair with lovely banana shampoo. Then Mr Monkey sat Lawrence in a special chair that rose up when he pumped it with his foot. Swoosh! As Lawrence went higher and higher, he spotted his friend Mike the Monkey reading a comic in the corner of the shop.

"Hi Mike," he giggled. "Are you here for a haircut too?"

"No," said Mike, and went back to his comic.

Mr Monkey started to comb Lawrence's mane. He lifted his scissors to start cutting – then he put them down again. He combed a bit more . . . and a bit more . . . and then he peered at the comb.

"Dear, oh dear," he said. "I think there is something alive in your mane, Lawrence."

"Wow! Let me see, Dad!" cried Mike, and he stood on his tiptoes trying to get a good look at Lawrence's mane.

Mr Monkey lowered the chair and whisked Lawrence to the door. "I think you should go home straight away, Lawrence, and tell your mother what I have found."

"OK," said Lawrence, and walked off, scratching his mane.

Lawrence was still scratching when he got home. Mrs Lion wasn't very pleased with his haircut. "It doesn't look like you've had your hair cut at all," she scolded.

"I didn't!" exclaimed Lawrence. "Mr Monkey said I had something living in my hair and he sent me home!"

"Something living in your hair?" shrieked Mrs Lion.
"Oh, how horrible!" She marched Lawrence straight
round to Doctor Spot's surgery.

13

"We want to see Doctor Spot," whispered Mrs Lion to the receptionist.

"What seems to be the problem?" asked the receptionist, rather too loudly for Mrs Lion's liking.

"My son can't stop scratching his mane and there seems to be something alive in it," Mrs Lion whispered again, looking round nervously at the other patients in the waiting room.

"Oh, he probably has head lice," announced the receptionist to the whole room. "I don't think he needs to see Doctor Spot. Miss Orang-utan the Practice Nurse can help you."

Miss Orang-utan showed Mrs Lion how to check for head lice. She parted Lawrence's mane and showed Mrs Lion some white blobs on the hair shafts.

"Those are not head lice," she explained. "They are nits, which are the egg sacs. These ones are white and quite easy to see, which means that the lice have already hatched and the sacs are empty."

"Gross!" said Lawrence. "Where do they go once they have hatched?"

"Well, it's very hard to tell on dry hair if the lice are still there," said Miss Orang-utan. "What you need to do is go home and wash your mane, and check it for lice when it is wet."

18

Mrs Lion took Lawrence home and followed Miss Orang-utan's instructions. First, she washed Lawrence's mane and put lots of hair conditioner on it which made it easier to comb. Then she took the special fine-toothed nit comb that Miss Orang-utan had given her, and combed through Lawrence's mane, section by section. Each time she finished a stroke, she checked the comb. Suddenly, she let out a huge shriek.

"Eeeeek! There's something moving. Oh, how horrid – it's a head louse!"

"Let me see!" cried Lawrence, excitedly. He peered at the comb. "Oooh, it doesn't look very friendly, does it?"

Mrs Lion covered Lawrence's mane with a special lotion that Miss Orang-utan had given her. It felt like ages before she washed it off.

"Are all the lice dead now?" asked Lawrence.

"I do hope so," said Mrs Lion, "but you may have eggs in your mane that will still hatch, so I will have to do all this again in a week's time."

"Humph!" said Lawrence, who had decided that head lice were a real nuisance.

"And I have to make a list of everyone who you have been near and they have to be checked too," sighed Mrs Lion.

Lawrence thought of his father's huge mane. He certainly hoped that the head lice hadn't moved in there, because it would take ages to get a comb through all that hair!

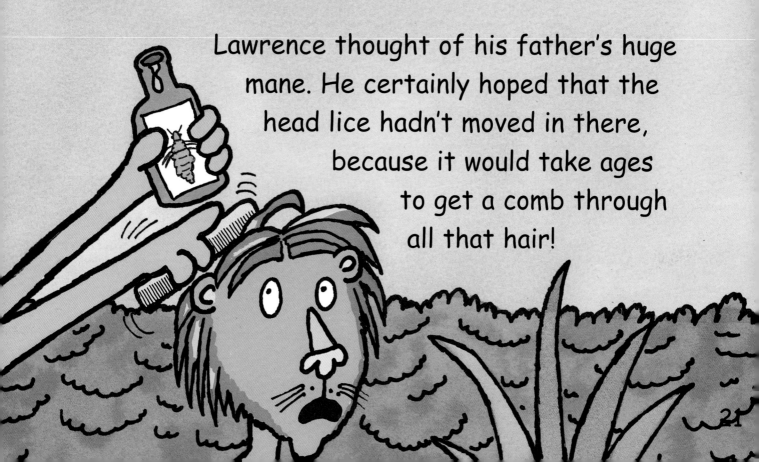

At school the next day, Mike was making trouble
for Lawrence. "Lawrence must have really dirty
hair to catch nits," he sneered. "Better stay well
away from him if you don't want to itch and
scratch all day long."

"MICHAEL MONKEY!" snapped Miss Flamingo, their teacher, who was standing behind Mike. She was very cross. "Absolutely anyone can catch head lice and it has nothing to do with how clean or dirty your hair is."

23

Miss Flamingo asked Doctor Spot to the school to talk to her class all about head lice. Doctor Spot drew a picture of a head louse on the blackboard. It had six tiny claws which it used to grip on to the hair once it had hatched. It didn't look very nice, and some of Lawrence's classmates felt a bit itchy just at the sight of it.

"How do you catch head lice, Doctor Spot?" asked Franklin the Frog.

"Well, they can't jump," said Doctor Spot. "They just walk from one head to another when your hair touches someone else's. Anyway, you have nothing to worry about, Franklin," he chuckled. "You don't have hair, so you can't get nits." Franklin looked rather pleased. So did Harriet the Hippopotamus and Ronnie the Rhino, who didn't have any hair either.

"Head lice can lay about 10 nits a day," explained Doctor Spot. "After a week, they hatch into lice. After another week, those head lice can start laying eggs of their own."

"Golly," said Gloria the Gorilla, who was very good at maths. "In a few weeks, you could have zillions of head lice in your hair."

"Well, not zillions," said Doctor Spot, "but they do multiply at quite a rate."

The young animals all started scratching their heads – even the ones with no hair! Then they all went home to tell their parents about their head lice lesson.

At school the next day, Mike the Monkey was very quiet. Lawrence sat behind him in class and was sure there was a smell of head-lice lotion from the desk in front. But Lawrence was much too nice to say anything – he just smiled quietly to himself.

Parents' pages: Nits

What are the symptoms?

An itchy scalp, caused by the head lice sucking blood through the scalp. Not everyone with head lice will experience itching, however.

How can I confirm my child has head lice?

- On dry hair, you can see nits (egg sacs) which are glued to the hair shaft. Once the egg has hatched, the sac is white and easier to see. They may look like dandruff, but will not comb out easily. It is very difficult to find head lice in dry hair as they not much bigger than a pin-head and hide as soon as the hair is disturbed. *Finding nits in your child's hair does not confirm that they have head lice.*
- Wash the hair and comb it through carefully with a fine-toothed nit comb (available from your pharmacy). Applying conditioner may make it easier to comb straight hair, or oil if your child has curly hair. Keep the comb in contact with the scalp for as long as possible. Check the comb for head lice after each stroke. If you find any living lice, you need to take action.

How can I treat my child for head lice?

Insecticidal treatments

- There are numerous insecticidal head lice treatments on the market. Ask your pharmacist or healthcare professional for advice, and follow the product instructions carefully.
- It is important to repeat the treatment 7 days later, because eggs may still hatch after the first treatment. Comb the hair carefully with a nit comb at each treatment.

Bug-busting

- This method aims to get rid of the lice by removing them with a nit comb. Wash and condition or oil the hair. Comb the hair carefully in sections with a nit comb, checking the comb for lice with each stroke. It may help to comb the hair over a white tissue so it is easier to see the lice. Continue for 30 minutes, and repeat twice a week for at least 2 weeks.
- Some people prefer an insecticide-free treatment, but bug-busting can be very time-consuming, especially if there are multiple family members to treat.

Can my child catch head lice again?

- Unfortunately, it's very easy to catch head lice again. That is why it is so important to make a list of anyone your child has been in contact with, so they can be checked for head lice too.

Doctor Spot says:

- Only treat your child if you find living head lice in their hair. Do not be tempted to treat them 'just in case'.
- Head lice may become resistant to insecticidal treatments. If you still find living lice after a second treatment, ask a healthcare professional for advice.
- Always consult a healthcare professional before using chemical treatments on someone who is either under 1 year of age, suffers from asthma or allergies, or is pregnant or breastfeeding.
- Inform your child's school that they have nits, and tell all friends and family, adults and children alike, who may have had head to head contact with your child.

Other titles in the series:

Harriet has Tonsillitis
ISBN: 1-902463-38-2
Harriet the Hippopotamus has a nasty case of tonsillitis at her best friend's birthday party. Luckily, Doctor Spot is at hand to make her feel better.

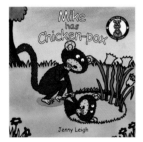

Mike has Chicken-pox
ISBN: 1-902463-38-2
Mike the Monkey comes out in spots and feels uncomfortably itchy. But he soon feels better when Doctor Spot prescribes a soothing lotion.

George has Meningitis
ISBN: 1-902463-91-9
George the Gorilla is feeling very ill. His sister, Gloria, learned about the tell-tale signs of meningitis at school, and gets her father to call in Doctor Spot without delay.

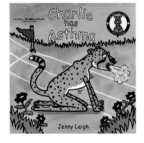

Charlie has Asthma
ISBN: 1-902463-68-4
Charlie the Cheetah finds he's always running out of breath. Doctor Spot tells him what's wrong and gives Charlie a special inhaler to help him breathe more easily.

Rachel has Eczema
ISBN: 1-902463-92-7
Rachel the Rhino is sore and itchy and can't sleep at night. Doctor Spot prescribes ointments and dressings which soon make her feel better.